# ROB GRONKOWSKI

Jon M. Fishman

Lerner Publications ◆ Minneapolis

Lerner Publications Company
A division of Lerner Publishing Group, Inc.
241 First Avenue North
Minneapolis, MN 55401 USA

For reading levels and more information, look up this title at www.lernerbooks.com.

Main body text set in Albany Std 15/22. Typeface provided by Agfa.

**Library of Congress Cataloging-in-Publication Data**

Names: Fishman, Jon M., author.
Title: Rob Gronkowski / Jon M. Fishman.
Description: Minneapolis : Lerner Publications, 2018. | Series: Sports All-Stars | Includes bibliographical references and index. | Audience: Age 7–11. | Audience: Grade 4 to 6. | Description based on print version record and CIP data provided by publisher; resource not viewed.
Identifiers: LCCN 2017005926 (print) | LCCN 2017011599 (ebook) | ISBN 9781512450897 (eb pdf) | ISBN 9781512439243 (lb : alk. paper) | ISBN 9781512456196 (pb : alk. paper)
Subjects: LCSH: Gronkowski, Rob, 1989– —Juvenile literature. | Football players—United States—Biography—Juvenile literature. | Tight ends (Football)—United States—Biography—Juvenile literature.
Classification: LCC GV939.G777 (ebook) | LCC GV939.G777 F57 2018 (print) | DDC 796.332092 [B]—dc23

LC record available at https://lccn.loc.gov/2017005926

Manufactured in the United States of America
1-42137-25410-4/13/2017

# CONTENTS

# PATRIOTS'
# DAY

Gronkowski runs for a touchdown!

**On October 30, 2016, Rob Gronkowski lined up against the Buffalo Bills in New York.** The crowd buzzed all around him. He had grown up in the Buffalo area. But Gronkowski didn't let the excitement of playing near his hometown get to him. The **tight end** focused on every play, every moment.

Gronkowski and the New England Patriots led the game in the second quarter, 14–10. That's when he broke loose for one of his best plays of the season. He raced down the middle of the field. Patriots quarterback Tom Brady hit him with a perfect pass.

Gronkowski was in the clear! The Buffalo defenders couldn't bring the big man down. After scoring a 53-yard touchdown, he bowed to the crowd and spiked the ball into the ground as hard as he could.

It was the 68th receiving touchdown of Gronkowski's National Football League (NFL) career. That made him the all-time team leader in touchdown catches. "[It's] definitely an honor to come home to my hometown and get that record," Gronkowski said. "To hold the record for most **franchise** touchdowns is just unbelievable."

The score gave New England a solid lead, but a lot of time was still left in the game. In the third quarter, Gronkowski ran toward the Buffalo defense. He turned

Gronkowski keeps the ball close as he runs for a touchdown.

Gronkowski's nickname in the NFL is Gronk. He also introduced fans to another word. Gronking is slamming the football into the ground as hard as you can in celebration.

left, then turned again and raced up the side of the field. Brady threw. Gronkowski got both of his hands on the ball and pulled it in. His feet danced near the sideline. The 18-yard catch helped the Patriots score another touchdown.

He was at it again in the fourth quarter. This time, Brady hit Gronkowski in the chest with the ball. The powerful tight end snatched it and turned up the field. A Buffalo defender stood in his way, but Gronkowski shoved him aside. Defenders pulled from behind, but he kept rumbling down the field. He ran 15 yards before the Bills were able to bring him to the ground. First down! New England kicked a **field goal** to take a huge lead. Thanks to Gronkowski's big day, they won the game, 41–25.

# THE BROTHERS GRONK

Rob (center) is the second youngest of five brothers. Here he poses with three of them.

**Robert Gronkowski was born on May 14, 1989, in Amherst, New York.** NFL fans know him as the best tight end in the league. But to fully understand his path to stardom, you have to go back in time almost 100 years.

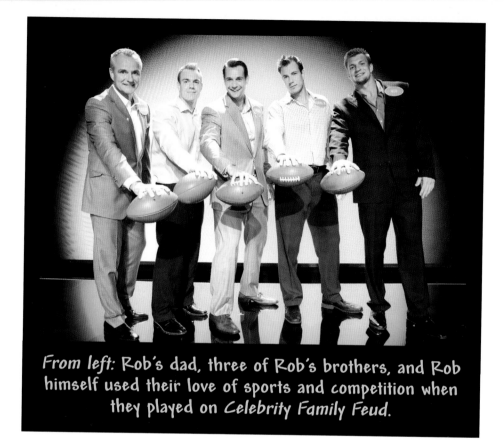

*From left: Rob's dad, three of Rob's brothers, and Rob himself used their love of sports and competition when they played on Celebrity Family Feud.*

In 1924, Ignatius Gronkowski raced in the Olympic Games in Paris, France. He was Rob Gronkowski's great-grandfather. Ignatius was a **cyclist**. He competed in long **road races**. He didn't win a medal, but he passed his love of sports on to his grandson and great-grandchildren.

Rob's father, Gordon, played on the **offensive line** at Syracuse University. He didn't make it to the NFL. But football was an important part of his life. He pushed his five boys to become athletes. Gordon Jr., Dan, Chris, Rob, and Glenn didn't need to be pushed hard. They loved to compete in hockey, football, baseball, and other sports.

Their father wanted his sons to receive **scholarships** for college. To do that, they would need to succeed in the classroom as well as on the field. "School's first no matter what," he told his sons. "Get educated, and then the sports."

The boys' mother, Diane, stayed home to care for her children while their father worked outside the home. She broke up fights, mended cuts, drove the boys to

Three of Rob's brothers also played in the NFL: Dan, Chris, and Glenn. His oldest brother, Gordon Jr., played professional baseball.

Rob Gronkowski and some of his family attended the 2015 ESPYs. From left: his dad, Gordon Sr.; brother Dan; Rob; his mom, Diane Walters; and brothers Chris and Gordon Jr.

games, and took care of them in hundreds of other ways. "Growing up as a kid, you really don't know all the stuff that moms put up with," Rob said. "We definitely drove her crazy."

By the time Rob was a high school senior in 2007, he stood 6 feet 6 (2 meters) tall. He weighed 240 pounds (109 kilograms). His hard work in class and on the field had paid off. **Scouts** ranked him as the fourth-best high school tight end in the United States. Rob had dozens of scholarship offers. He decided to attend the University of Arizona.

In 2007 and 2008, Gronkowski scored 16 touchdowns in 22 games with the Arizona Wildcats. He planned to leave college for the NFL after the 2009 season. But before the Wildcats' first game, he hurt his back lifting weights. He had surgery and missed the entire season.

He worked to return to the field. Instead of playing football and having fun with his friends, he did **rehab** exercises. His hard work paid off again. His back fully healed. In 2010, he entered the NFL Draft. The New England Patriots chose him with the 42nd overall pick, and an NFL star was born.

Gronkowski was interviewed by the NFL Network after being drafted by the New England Patriots.

Gronkowski poses with a Patriots helmet after being selected in the 2010 NFL Draft.

Rob (right) practices blocking during training with Patriots teammate LaAdrian Waddle (left).

**When Rob was a kid, playing sports was just for fun.** He loved to compete with his brothers and friends. As the boys became teenagers, their father convinced them to take it more seriously. "If you want to keep pursuing sports, you need to start training," he said.

The family had weights and a space to work out in the basement. First, Dan started training. Then Gordon Jr. followed his younger brother. Chris, Rob, and Glenn soon followed too. Before long, the brothers were pushing one another to get bigger and stronger.

Rob, his brothers, and CEO of Town Sports International, Patrick Walsh, spike footballs after their first workout in a space called the Gronk Zone at Boston Sports Club.

To warm up before a workout, the brothers play basketball. They take turns shooting. When one of them misses a shot, they run to the end of the court and back. This loosens their muscles and gets their hearts pumping faster.

Next, they hit the weights. **Dumbbell** and **barbell** exercises are a big part of their workouts. They also do lots of push-ups. To cool down afterward, the Gronkowskis jump into the pool to swim some laps and splash around.

Swimming is a good **cardio** workout. To get ready for the NFL season, Gronkowski also does **sprints**. He runs 100 yards as fast as he can 10 times. He keeps working until he can run 100 yards 20 times. He often does this *before* lifting weights! Gronkowski keeps the

Gronkowski runs sprints during warm-ups.

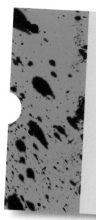

Gronkowski doesn't always stick to his healthful diet. Sometimes he treats himself to a pepperoni pizza or a steak-and-cheese sub sandwich.

cardio workout going on a rowing machine. The rowing motion strengthens his lungs and muscles.

Gronkowski learned from his parents to eat healthful food to fuel his workouts. They fed their boys chicken and vegetables and other wholesome meals. They went through a *lot* of food. The family spent hundreds of dollars a week on groceries and drank almost 3 gallons (11 liters) of milk every day. To keep all that food fresh, the family had four refrigerators—one in the kitchen and three in the garage!

To help keep his body in NFL shape, Gronkowski makes sure his meals include certain foods. He always has a green vegetable such as broccoli. Strawberries or blueberries are also on the menu. For **protein**, he likes to have chicken or tuna. The healthful food gives him plenty of energy to have fun on and off the field.

# FUN, FOOTBALL, AND FAMILY

Gronkowski spikes the ball after scoring a touchdown.

**Rob Gronkowski loves to have a good time.** Whether he's spiking the ball into the ground after a touchdown or goofing around with fans, he always looks as if he's having fun. That's one of the reasons he appears on TV so often.

*Crashletes* is a kids' TV show that plays videos of sports bloopers.

He's been on almost every major talk show, from *Good Morning America* to *The Tonight Show Starring Jimmy Fallon*. Maybe you saw him at the Nickelodeon Kids' Choice Awards or on *Crashletes*, the sports show he hosts.

In 2015, Gronkowski appeared on *Celebrity Family Feud* with his brothers Dan, Chris, and Gordon Jr., and their father. The Gronkowskis lost the charity game, but they still had a great time. They danced, answered fun questions, and joked with host Steve Harvey.

What would Gronkowski do if he didn't play in the **NFL**? He may have been a professional wrestler. He is good friends with wrestler Mojo Rawley. "I love watching him," Gronkowski said. The two have talked about getting Gronkowski into the ring. He says he'll do it—if he can body-slam his friend. Gronkowski says his wrestling name would be the Gronk.

Mojo Rawley and Gronkowski (right) like to goof off and have fun together.

Gronkowski has also appeared in countless commercials. He has been in ads for companies such as Dunkin' Donuts and Nike. He was also on the cover of the *Madden NFL 17* video game.

When he's not playing on the field, Rob enjoys playing video games.

Gronkowski signed a new **contract** in 2012. The Patriots agreed to pay him $54 million, the most money for a tight end in NFL history. He says he hasn't spent any of it. He gets by with the money he makes from commercials, and he doesn't spend a lot. In fact, he says he still wears his "favorite pair of jeans from high school."

In 2016, the Patriots nominated Gronkowski for the Walter Payton NFL Man of the Year award. Each season, the NFL gives the award to a player who helps his team and his community. The Gronk Nation Youth Foundation helps young people stay healthy and succeed in school and in sports.

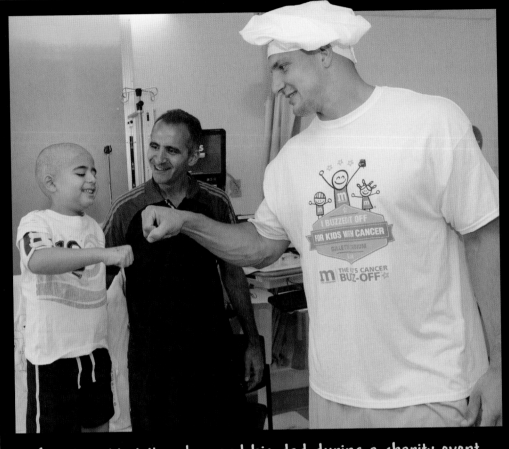

Gronkowski visits a boy and his dad during a charity event.

Gronkowski also works with groups such as the Make-A-Wish Foundation to meet young football fans. He loves to visit schools in the New England area. "It's all smiles, the whole school going crazy, everyone going wild," Gronkowski said. "When it's like that, it is fun for [everybody]."

In 2014, Gronkowski met with patients at Boston Children's Hospital.

# SUPER GRONK

Gronkowski soars through the air as he tries to avoid Broncos players on the field.

**Scouts weren't quite sure what to make of Gronkowski when he entered the NFL Draft in 2010.** He hadn't played football in more than a year due to his back injury in college. Would he be able to stay healthy in the NFL where the players are bigger, faster, and stronger?

Gronkowski was happy to
be drafted by the Patriots.

The Cincinnati Bengals weren't convinced Gronkowski was the best tight end in the draft. They chose tight end Jermaine Gresham in the first round. In fact, every team that had a first-round pick passed on Gronkowski. Even the Patriots picked someone else.

Finally, New England snatched him in the second round. He scored 10 touchdowns in his first season and proved that he should have been chosen sooner. In 2011, he led the NFL with 17 receiving touchdowns. He was voted to the **Pro Bowl** for the first time.

Gronkowski makes a catch during Super Bowl XLIX.

In 2015, Gronkowski played in the biggest game of his life: Super Bowl XLIX. He caught six passes and a touchdown to help New England beat the Seattle Seahawks, 28–24. He had gone from lifting weights in his basement with his brothers to world champion. With his family supporting him every step of the way, the fun is just getting started for Gronkowski.

Gronkowski celebrates after the Patriots win Super Bowl XLIX.

a powerful grip like steel. He can even run pretty well for a man his size. Put it all together, and you've got a touchdown-scoring machine.

## Most Receiving Touchdowns in NFL History*

| | |
|---|---|
| Rob Gronkowski | 68 |
| Stanley Morgan | 67 |
| Ben Coates | 50 |
| Randy Moss | 50 |
| Gino Cappelletti | 42 |
| Jim Colclough | 39 |
| Irving Fryar | 38 |
| Wes Welker | 37 |
| Troy Brown | 31 |
| Russ Francis | 28 |

*Through the 2016 regular season

# Source Notes

6   Jonah Bronstein, "New England Patriots TE Rob Gronkowski Sets Team Touchdown Record," UPI, October 31, 2016, http://www.upi .com/Sports_News/NFL/2016/10/31/New-England-Patriots-TE-Rob -Gronkowski-sets-team-touchdown-record/9301477920334/.

10   Bruce Weber, "How Rob Gronkowski's Dad Raised America's First Family of Jocks," *Vanity Fair*, December 9, 2015, http://www .vanityfair.com/culture/2015/12/rob-gronkowski-first-family-of-sports.

11   Craig Handel, "Gronkowskis' Mother, a Fort Myers Resident, Raised Some Big Boys," *News-Press.com*, last modified May 7, 2016, http://www.news-press.com/story/sports/college/football/2016/05/06 /gronkowskis-mother-fort-myers-resident-raised-some-big -boys/83871050/.

15   Weber, "Rob Gronkowski's Dad."

20   Anthony DiMoro, "Rob Gronkowski Eyeing WWE Career after Retirement from NFL," *Forbes*, May 24, 2016, http://www.forbes .com/sites/anthonydimoro/2016/05/24/rob-gronkowski-eyeing-wwe -career-after-retirement-from-nfl/#76a2d828293c.

21   Blake Oestriecher, "Rob Gronkowski's Money Management Should Be a Lesson for All Pro Athletes," *Forbes*, June 23, 2015, http://www.forbes.com/sites/blakeoestriecher/2015/06/23/rob -gronkowskis-money-management-should-be-a-lesson-for-all-pro -athletes/#74231b5839fb.

22   Mike Reiss, "The Rob Gronkowski Story Not Often Told: Generosity to Charitable Causes," *ESPN*, November 5, 2015, http://www .espn.com/blog/new-england-patriots/post/_/id/4787119/the-rob -gronkowski-story-not-often-told-generosity-to-charitable-causes.

# Glossary

**barbell:** long bars with weights at each end

**cardio:** a workout designed to strengthen the heart and lungs

**contract:** an agreement between a player and a team that states how much a player will be paid and how long he will play for the team

**cyclist:** a person who rides bicycles

**dumbbell:** short bars with weights at each end

**field goal:** a kick that goes between the goalposts at either end of the field. A field goal is worth three points.

**franchise:** a team and the organization around it, including the owner, ticket sellers, and others

**offensive line:** the five players at the front of the offense whose main job is to block defenders

**Pro Bowl:** the NFL all-star game

**protein:** a substance found in foods (such as meat and beans) that is an important part of the human diet

**rehab:** short for *rehabilitation*, or the process of returning to health

**road races:** races that take place on roads people use every day

**scholarships:** money awarded to students to help pay for school

**scouts:** people who judge the skills of athletes

**sprints:** short distance runs done as fast as possible

**tight end:** a player who usually lines up at one end of the offensive line and either blocks or catches passes

Braun, Eric. *Tom Brady*. Minneapolis: Lerner Publications, 2017.

Gronk Nation Youth Foundation
http://gronknation.com/foundation

Kelley, K. C. *Rob Gronkowski*. New York: Bearport, 2016.

New England Patriots
http://www.patriots.com

NFL RUSH
http://www.nflrush.com

Savage, Jeff. *Football Super Stats*. Minneapolis: Lerner Publications, 2018.

# Index

# Photo Acknowledgments

The images in this book are used with the permission of: © iStockphoto.com/63151 (gold and silver stars); © Diamond Images/Getty Images, p. 2; © Brett Carlsen/ Getty Images, p. 4; © Barry Chin/The Boston Globe/Getty Images, p. 6; © Allen Berezovsky/Getty Images, p. 8; Adam Taylor/© ABC/Getty Images, p. 9; © Steve Granitz/WireImage/Getty Images, p. 11; AP Photo/Ben Liebenberg, p. 12; AP Photo/ Jason DeCrow, p. 13; AP Photo/Steven Senne, p. 14; © Scott Eisen/Getty Images, p. 15; © Stacy Revere/Getty Images, p. 16; © Kevin Hoffman/USA TODAY Sports, p. 18; © Nickelodeon/Courtesy Everett Collection, p. 19; STARPICZ/Splash News/ Newscom, p. 20; © Stephen Lovekin/Getty Images, p. 21; © Darren McCollester/ Getty Images, pp. 22, 23; © Ezra Shaw/Getty Images, p. 24; AP Photo/Frank Franklin II, p. 25; © Christian Petersen/Getty Images, p. 26; AP Photo/Tom Hauck, p. 27.

Front cover: © Diamond Images/Getty Images, © iStockphoto.com/neyro2008 (motion lines).